Welcome to my 3rd book of poems. This time we will cover emotions. Thank you for reading!

Happiness

In realms of rapture, where ecstasy thrives,
Extreme happiness in jubilant dives. A
symphony of emotions, wild and untamed,
Where hearts ignite, unbridled and
unclaimed.

It soars on the wings of euphoric delight, A
kaleidoscope of colors, oh, what a sight! Like
fireworks bursting in a celestial show,
Extreme happiness, an ethereal glow.

In laughter's cascade, and tears of pure glee,
A torrent of bliss, an ocean running free.
Exhilaration pulses, electric and alive, A
fervent crescendo, where passions strive.

Disgust

In the realm of repulsion, I behold, A succinct
tale of disgust, untold. Like bile rising, it
clenches the gut, A torrent of aversion, fierce
and uncut.

It thrives in sights that make eyes wince,
From decaying matter to a putrid rinse. Each
grotesque image, a dagger to the mind,
Provoking shudders, leaving reason behind.

With a touch so repulsive, it leaves a stain,
An icy residue that won't wane. The clammy,
the slimy, the things unclean, Evoke a recoil,
a shiver unforeseen.

Disgust's symphony resounds in the ear, A
discordant chorus of dread and fear. The
grating cacophony of loathing's call, Pierces
the soul, making senses enthrall.

It leaves a taste, bitter and vile, A rancid
flavor, hard to reconcile. A grim reminder
that repulsion clings, And lingers on the
palate, where bitterness sings.

Love

In the realm of emotions, love takes flight, A radiant warmth, a beacon of light. It blossoms within, like a gentle flame, Igniting the heart, forever the same.

Love's touch is tender, a soothing caress, Filling our souls with pure happiness. It wraps us in comfort, like a soft embrace, Melting our worries, leaving no trace.

With love, the world transforms, becomes anew, Colors grow brighter, skies a deeper blue. It paints our lives with hues of joy and grace, Creating a haven, a sacred space.

Embarrasment

Oh, how it scorns and gnaws within, A torment vile, a serpent's sin. Each stuttered word, each awkward glance, A symphony of mortals' dance.

Yet, let not shame forever bind, For laughter heals, and time is kind. Embrace the flaws that make us real, And rise above, with grace and zeal.

For in the depths of our despair, We find the strength to truly care. So let embarrassment take its flight, And bask in our imperfect light.

Annoyance

In the realm of vexation, annoyance takes
flight, A tempest of irritation, a relentless
plight. It tiptoes on patience, like a
delicate thread, Igniting frustration with
each word left unsaid.

It lingers in moments, both big and small,
A persistent murmur, a dissonant call.
Like a pebble in the shoe, it nags and it
pokes, Testing our composure until it
evokes

A symphony of sighs, a chorus of unrest,
Yet amidst the annoyance, we mustn't be
oppressed. For in the depths of
irritation's abyss, We find strength to rise,
and frustration dismiss.

Surprise

Surprise, a spark that sets the soul alight,
Unveiling mysteries in a flash of light. It
sweeps through our veins with a thrilling
grace, A whirlwind of emotions we
cannot erase.

From the mundane routine, it springs
forth, A delightful interruption, giving life
its worth. A symphony of gasps, mixed
with awe, As surprise paints colors we
never foresaw.

Conflicting sensations in a delicate blend,
A rollercoaster ride with no foreseeable
end. The heart races wildly, uncertainty
unfurls, Surprise, a reminder that life still
swirls.

Envy

Within shadows cast by dreams, a poison blooms,

Envy's tendrils slither, their silent looms.

In eyes aflame, a twisted dance unfolds,

The heart's blackened whispers, a tale untold.

Like venomous vines, they coil and squeeze,

Devouring souls, infecting with ease.

Beneath the surface, a festering storm,

Where envy's allure takes wicked form.

The seeds of discontent, envy sows,

And jealousy's fire relentlessly grows.

In this dark abyss, hearts beat as one,

Consumed by envy, all hope is undone.

Through secret glances, envy takes its toll,

A sinister hunger that devours the soul.

In hearts once pure, it breeds discontent,

Leaving scars of bitterness, deep and intent.

Like a venomous serpent, envy slithers,

Leaving behind ruins and shattered whispers.

With burning eyes, it seeks to destroy,

Everything sacred, every ounce of joy.

Cringe

In the depths of awkwardness, I find, A
cringe that grips both heart and mind. A
shiver down the spine, it crawls, When social
grace takes sudden falls.

A cringe, a pang of deep dismay, When
words misspeak, in disarray. Faces flushed
with burning shame, Oh, how I long to
change the game.

Satisfaction

In the stillness of a tranquil eve, A gentle whisper, a sigh to perceive. A heart at peace, contentment's embrace, A symphony of joy, serenity's grace.

With every goal achieved, a flame ignites, A blaze of triumph, soaring to new heights. The soul alights, a radiant glow, A dance of fulfillment, in rhythms that flow.

Frustration

In shadows deep, frustration weaves its tale,
A tempest's fury, an endless wail. With
clenched fists and furrowed brow, I battle
the currents that pull me low.

In the labyrinth of unmet desires, My dreams
entangled in thorny wires. A symphony of
hopes, elusive and vague, Frustration's grip,
a relentless plague.

Yet through the storm, a flicker of light, A
whisper of strength, a beacon in sight. With
resilience as my sword and shield, I'll rise
above, refusing to yield.

Affection

In the realm of tender hearts, where emotions dance, Affection blossoms, a sweet and gentle trance. It whispers softly, like a soothing breeze, Caressing souls with its heartfelt ease.

A gentle touch, a knowing gaze, Affection weaves its tender ways. It wraps us in its warm embrace, Filling every corner, every sacred space.

A symphony of love, it plays its tune, Resonating deeply, like a precious rune. With every beat, our spirits soar, Affection's magic, forevermore.

Worry

In the depths of worry's somber embrace,
Anxious thoughts whirl in a frenzied
chase. Like storm clouds gathering
overhead, Unease consumes, a heavy
thread.

Heart races, a drumbeat of fear, Doubt
whispers, "What if?" in my ear.

Jealousy

In the labyrinth of tangled emotion's play,
Jealousy emerges, fierce and astray. A
searing fire, consuming hearts with ire, A
serpent's tongue that whispers envy's desire.

It twists and turns, a venomous vine,
Distorting perceptions, poisoning the mind. A
cruel companion, it holds us in its sway, As
we watch others bask in fortune's ray.

Loathing

In the depths of my soul, a loathing resides,
A venomous flame that within me abides. It
gnaws at my spirit with relentless disdain,
Filling my heart with an unyielding pain.

The taste of bitterness lingers on my tongue,
As I wander through shadows, my spirit
undone. Each breath I take is heavy with
disgust, A relentless torment, in which I'm
thrust.

Oh, loathing, you wretched and cruel foe,
You pierce my heart, and it's hard to let go.

Anger

In the abyss of rage, a tempest howls,
Unleashing havoc, as darkness prowls. A
furious tempest, consuming all, Burning
bridges down, making walls fall.

The fury boils, a cauldron of wrath, A
seething volcano, ready to blast. Every fiber
screams, every nerve ignites, An inferno
within, devouring the night.

No reasoning prevails, just blind disdain,
Anguish and bitterness coursing through my
veins. The world turns bitter, as resentment
thrives, Every breath, a battle, as anger
survives.

Sadness

In the depths of sorrow's endless well,
Aching echoes of a heart that fell. Pain, a
relentless visitor to my soul, Its icy grip
leaves me feeling cold.

An empty void consumes my being, No
solace found in the world I'm seeing. Tears
cascade like a river of despair, Silent
screams, burdens I must bear.

In sadness' grasp, I find no reprieve, Aching,
longing, a desperate need to believe.

Fear

In the depths of darkness, fear takes hold, A
haunting presence, chilling and bold. It wraps
around the heart, squeezing tight, Filling the
mind with an endless night.

A whispering wind, a shiver down the spine,
Fear dances like shadows, a sinister sign. It
paralyzes courage, feeds on doubt, Leaving
no escape, no way to break out.

Anxiety

In the shadows of my restless mind, Anxiety's tendrils silently unwind. A symphony of worries, a haunting refrain, Engulfing my thoughts with relentless strain.

Like a tempest raging deep within, Anxiety's grip holds tight, under my skin. A dance of unease, an unyielding tide, Threatening to drown me, from deep inside.

Loneliness

Loneliness is an all-encompassing emotion, weaving its way through the fabric of one's being. It is a desolate landscape where the heart wanders aimlessly, yearning for connection and understanding. It is an ache, an emptiness that cannot be filled by mere presence. Loneliness whispers its melancholic tune, reminding us of our isolation, amplifying the silence that surrounds us. It seeps into every corner of our existence, casting a shadow over even the brightest moments. In its grip, we become spectators to the lives of others, longing for a sense of belonging, desperate for a meaningful connection that seems forever elusive. Loneliness can feel like an invisible weight, suffocating and isolating, as we navigate a world that seems indifferent to our presence. It engulfs us, leaving us feeling small, insignificant, and longing for the warmth of companionship.

Guilt

In shadows cast by deeds undone, Guilt's
burden weighs, my heart undone. Five souls
departed, lost in strife, Their absence cuts,
like jagged knife.

Oh, heavy guilt, my constant guide,
Remorseful tears, I cannot hide. I carry the
weight of their demise, Haunted by echoes
of their cries.

Thank you

Kustantaja: BoD – Books on Demand, Helsinki, Suomi
Valmistaja: BoD – Books on Demand, Norderstedt, Saksa
ISBN: 978-952-80-0696-1